MACHINES IN ACTION

SCREWS

ANGELA ROYSTON

Heinemann Library
Chicago, Illinois

© 2001 Reed Educational & Professional Publishing
Published by Heinemann Library,
an imprint of Reed Educational & Professional Publishing,
100 N. LaSalle, Suite 1010
Chicago, IL 60602
Customer Service 888-454-2279
Visit our website at www.heinemannlibrary.com

Designed by Visual Image
Illustrations by Barry Atkinson
Originated by Dot Gradations
Printed in Hong Kong/China

05 04 03 02 01

10 9 8 7 6 5 4 3 2 1

Library of Congress Cataloging-in-Publication Data

Royston, Angela.
　　Screws / Angela Royston.
　　　　　p. cm. – (Machines in action)
　　Includes bibliographical references and index.
　　ISBN 1-57572-322-0 (library)
　　1. Screws—Juvenile literature. [1. Screws.] I. Title. II. Series.

TJ1338 .R69 2000
621.8'82—dc21

00-029592

Acknowledgments

The author and publishers are grateful to the following for permission to reproduce copyright material:
Cumulus / Trevor Clifford, pp. 8, 10, 12, 15, 16; Ecoscene / Ayres, p. 21; Heinemann / Trevor Clifford, pp. 4, 9, 11, 13, 14, 17, 20, 28, 29; J. Allan Cash Photo Library, p. 24; Pictor Uniphoto, p. 27; Robert Harding Picture Library / J. Lightfoot, pp. 6, 23; Skyscan Photolibrary / Chris Allan, p. 26; Tony Stone Images /Robert Frerck, p. 7; TRH Pictures / P&O p. 25.

Cover photograph reproduced with permission of Science Photo Library.

Every effort has been made to contact copyright holders of any material reproduced in this book. Any omissions will be rectified in subsequent printings if notice is given to the publisher.

Some words are shown in bold, **like this.** You can find out what they mean by looking in the glossary.

CONTENTS

What Is a Screw?

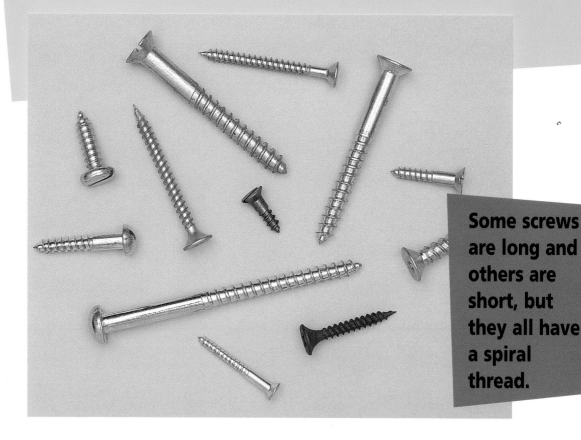

Some screws are long and others are short, but they all have a spiral thread.

Screws are used to join one thing to another. Look around you. You may not notice many screws right away, but look closer. The legs of chairs and tables are often screwed on. Door **hinges** are screwed into the door frame. Different parts of television sets, computers, and cars are screwed together too.

Did you know?

Screws were first used instead of nails about 500 years ago, but the first known screw was invented over 2,200 years ago by a Greek mathematician named Archimedes. He invented a huge screw that lifted water from one level to another.

The easiest way to get a heavy load to the top of the hill is to pull it up the slope. You have to pull it farther but it takes less effort than lifting it straight up off the ground. A screw is a kind of slope.

A simple machine

A screw is a simple machine. The most common kind of screw has a flat head, a thin thread, and a sharp point at the end. The thread is a slope which winds around in a **spiral**. With a lot of turning but a small amount of **effort** you can produce a lot of **force**.

A screw is so simple, you may not think of it as a machine. Levers, wheels, springs, ramps, and pulleys are also simple machines. This book will show you how useful screws are. It looks at how different kinds of screws work and how we use them.

Spirals

A **spiral** is a slope which moves up and around in a circle. A screw works because it has a spiral thread, but other things use spirals too. Multi-story parking garages often have a curved slope for cars to drive from one floor to another. The curve makes a long, gentle slope that is easy to drive up and down.

This water slide is in the shape of a spiral. You slide around and around the slope and splash into the pool at the bottom. You slide around a long way to drop a short distance.

Spiral staircase

A spiral staircase has more steps than a ladder of the same height. The shallower the step the easier it is to climb. In a spiral staircase, you walk a long way around to climb a short way up.

A spiral staircase takes up much less space than a long, straight flight of stairs so it is usually used where there is not much space. Round towers and lighthouses, for example, have spiral staircases.

Try this!

Turn a straight slope into a spiral. Cut a square of paper in half along the diagonal, to give you a triangle. Place a pencil along one of the shorter sides of the triangle. Roll the paper around the pencil towards the opposite corner. The long side of the triangle makes a spiral around the pencil.

Lids and Tops

The spiral thread inside the cap of the bottle exactly fits over the spiral thread at the top of the bottle.

A screw cap or lid makes a tight **seal**. The **spiral** screw on the bottle fits into the spiral groove inside the top. The screw pulls the lid down onto the seal. It fits so tightly that no liquid can leak out.

A bottle of soda has a screw cap to keep the fizz inside from escaping. After you have poured a drink you must screw the cap back on to keep the drink from going flat. You turn the cap a long way around to push the lid down a short way.

Make it work!

Some bottles have a cork instead of a cap. The cork is slightly wider than the top of the bottle. When it is pushed into the bottle it is pressed tightly against the glass. Try to push a cork back into a bottle. Which is easier—pushing in the cork or screwing on a cap?

Each of these jars has a screw-on lid. The screw makes a tight fit which helps keep the food inside fresh.

Jars

Many jars have screw lids. The lid makes an **airtight** seal to keep the food inside clean and fresh. If jam is not sealed, it dries out and may get **moldy**. If coffee is not sealed, it loses some of its flavor. What do you think might happen to the pickles if the lid is loose?

Nuts and Bolts

Nuts and bolts are used to hold things together. They join the wheels to a bicycle, and they sometimes hold the different bars of a jungle gym together. Nuts and bolts are so strong that they are used to hold the engine in place inside a car.

A nut and bolt join the wheel to the bicycle frame. A wrench is used to tighten the nut.

The nut and bolt both have a **spiral** thread, like a screw bottle top. The bolt is pushed through the two holes in the bars of the frame, and the nut is screwed on tightly.

10

Think about it!

The size of a nut must match the size of the bolt. Which bolt would fit the large nut on the bottom right? Which bolt would fit the wing nut above it?

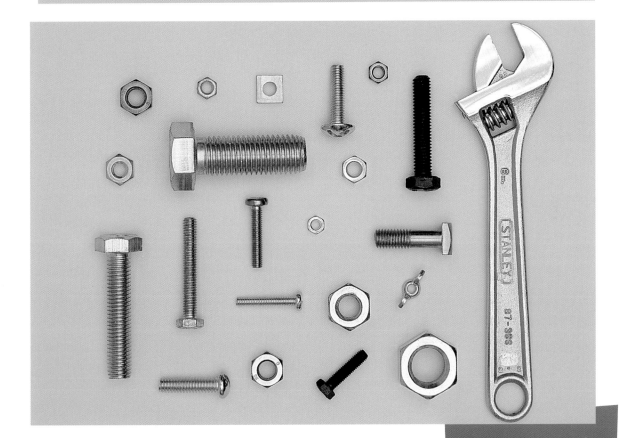

Wrench

Some nuts have wings on each side to help you turn them by hand, but most nuts are tightened with a **wrench**. The wrench is a lever that fits over the nut. The longer the wrench, the easier it is to turn the nut. Some wrenches can be adjusted to fit the size of any nut. Look at the wrench in this photo. Can you see how to adjust the size?

The outside of the nut can be any shape, but most are **hexagonal**. Why do you think that is so?

11

Screwdrivers and Corkscrews

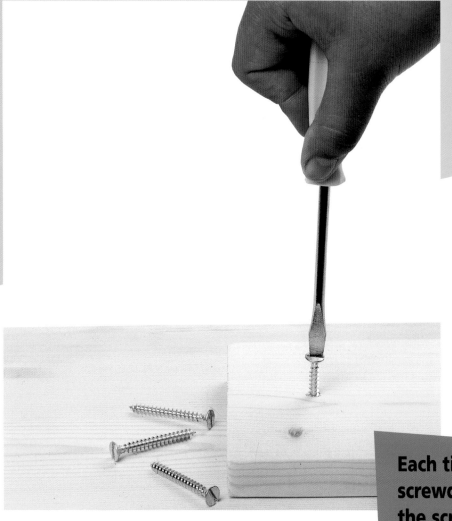

You cannot push a screw into hard wood using just your fingers. You have to use a **screwdriver**. The tip of the screwdriver fits into a slot or a small cross carved into the top, or head, of the screw. As you turn the screwdriver, it grips the screw and makes it turn, too. As the screw turns, the sharp thread cuts a spiral groove in the wood. The thread grips the groove tightly.

12

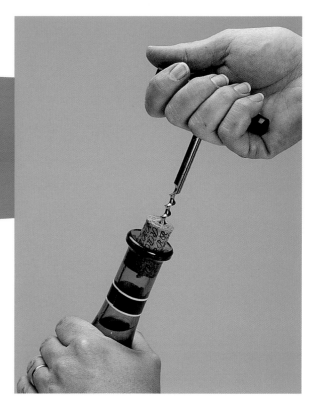

A cork fits tightly inside the neck of the bottle. To get the cork out, you have to twist a corkscrew into the cork and then pull hard!

Magnifying effort

A screwdriver magnifies your **effort**. The effort you put into turning the handle is concentrated on the tip of the screwdriver. And the **force** applied to the head of the screw is turned into an even bigger force at the point of the screw.

A corkscrew works like a screw and screwdriver combined. As you turn the handle of the corkscrew, the screw cuts a deep groove in the cork. The screw grips the cork all along the groove. When you pull the handle up, the cork slips out with a pop of air!

Make it work!

Use a spare piece of soft wood, some screws, and a screwdriver. Try to push the screw into the wood with your fingers. Now use the screwdriver. How far into the wood can you drive the screw? Be careful—the end of a screwdriver can be sharp.

13

Screws Are Strong

Each screw is only 1 inch long, but together the screws can hold up these shelves of books.

Screws are incredibly strong. Several small screws can hold up a shelf of books. The screws are short, but each one grips the wall so tightly the heavy weight of books will not pull them out. A few screws can take the weight of a heavy door, thick curtains, a large mirror, or a cupboard. Look to see what is hanging by a few screws in your home.

Vises and clamps are used in workshops to grip pieces of wood and other things. The handle turns the screw until the jaws of the vise or clamp press tightly against the wood.

Vises and clamps

A **vise** uses a screw to hold things firmly. For example, a vise can hold wood completely steady while it is being sawed. A vise can also hold a piece of metal steady while it is bent or hammered. The vise has two jaws. Turning the handle turns the screw to move one jaw toward the other.

A clamp works in the same way as a vise. Shoe menders use clamps when they glue a new sole to a shoe. The clamp presses the two parts together while the glue dries.

Think about it!

Why do you think most screws are made of metal? What would happen if a screw was made of wax or plaster?

Changing a Tire

All cars carry a spare tire and a bag of tools in case one of the tires goes flat. When that happens, the tools are used to change the tire. First the car has to be lifted using a car **jack**.

A small jack can lift one side of a car. As the handle turns the screw, the arm of the jack lifts up, taking the car with it.

The jack fits into a special plate under the car, and a handle is attached to the end of the screw. You have to turn the handle many times to lift the car just a little. In fact, the handle moves about 50 times farther than the car!

The wheel is attached to the car by four bolts and nuts. The nuts are screwed on so tightly you often need a big wrench to loosen them.

Lug nuts

Once the tire is off the ground, it can be removed. Each wheel is held on by four or five nuts and bolts, called lug nuts. The nuts are so tight it can take a lot of **effort** to loosen them, even with the car's special **wrench**. When the old tire is off, the spare tire is screwed on tight. The jack is wound down, and the car is ready to go.

Make it work!

Draw a design for a machine that can lift something heavy. What simple machines will you include to make your new design work?

Water Tap

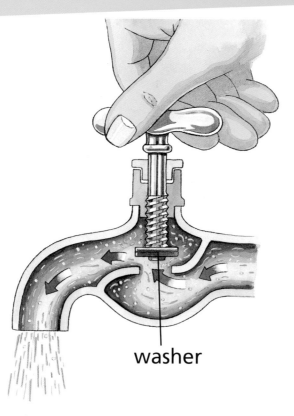

washer

How many times a day do you turn on a tap to get some water? When you have a bath, you turn the taps all the way and the water pours out. To wash your hands or get a drink of water, you turn the tap a little to let the water flow more slowly.

Try this!

Feel for yourself how powerful a tap and washer are. Turn on a tap or garden hose and put your thumb over the spout. Can you stop the water from flowing? The screw in the tap can!

How a tap works

The handle of the tap is joined to a large screw with a round, rubber disk on the end. The disk is called a **washer**. Turning the handle turns the screw and moves the washer up and down. The washer is like a plug which fits over a hole inside the tap.

When the washer is up, water flows through the hole and out of the tap. As you turn the tap off, the washer begins to block the hole, and the water flows more slowly. The water stops flowing only when the washer blocks the hole completely.

washer

When you turn the tap off, the screw pushes the rubber washer into the hole in the pipe to hold back the water.

Drills and Borers

As the drill bit spins around, the sharp point bites into the wood. The wider the drill bit, the wider the hole.

Drills are used to bore holes in wood, metal, plastic, and even the ground. A drill has a sharp point on a spiral screw called a **drill bit.** As the drill bit turns, the point breaks up the material to bore the hole. The loose material is pushed along the **spiral** out of the hole.

An electric drill spins fast and works quickly. Most people use an electric drill when they want to screw something into the wall. If you tried to fix a screw straight into a **plasterboard** wall, the plaster would crumble. Instead the drill makes a hole which is filled with a plastic plug. The screw is then driven into the plug.

This huge drill is called a pile driver. It is drilling a deep hole to make concrete foundations for a building.

Borers

Huge machines called borers and pile drivers dig deep holes through the ground. The huge screw on the end is called an **auger**. As the engine turns the auger, it breaks up the earth and the spiral screw fills with mud. The auger is then lifted up to the surface. It spins again and the mud flies off.

Did you know?

Huge drills bore through soil and thick layers of rock to reach oil trapped deep below the ground. These drills may burrow 25,000 feet (7,000 meters) through the rocks. This is nearly as deep as the height of the world's highest mountains.

Boring a Tunnel

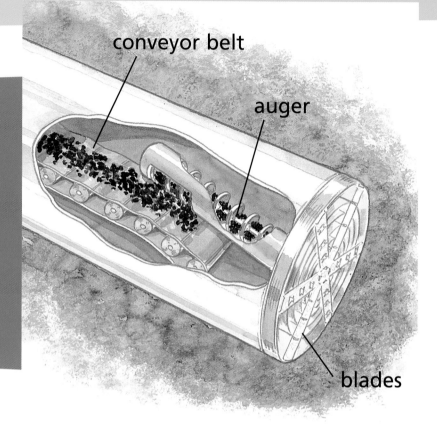

conveyor belt

auger

blades

A mechanical mole tunnels through soil and soft rock. The loose material passes onto a spinning auger that carries it up to a conveyor belt.

Most cities have tunnels deep below the ground that carry away waste water from buildings and the streets. Even bigger tunnels have been bored to carry roads and railways through mountains such as the Alps in Switzerland and the Rocky Mountains in North America.

Tunnel borers are huge machines that cut through soil and rocks to dig tunnels. Sharp blades at the front of a tunnel borer spin around and cut through the rock like a giant drill. As the machine inches forward, the loose rock and earth is passed back through the blades and onto a **conveyor belt**.

22

The Channel Tunnel

The Channel Tunnel was bored through rock under the sea between France and Britain. You can now travel by train from London to Paris. Huge machines bored the two main railway tunnels. Each machine was longer than two soccer fields and moved forward about one yard (one meter) every hour.

This kind of machine helped to bore the Channel Tunnel under the sea. Huge blades at the front of the machine cut through the rock. The broken rock passes through the blades straight onto a conveyor belt which loads it onto a train.

Did you know?

The world's longest transportation tunnel is the Seikan rail tunnel. It is 33¼ miles (53.8 kilometers) long and travels under the sea to link the Japanese islands of Honshu and Hokkaido.

Water Screws

An Archimedes screw is a kind of **pump**. Inside is an **auger**. As the handle is turned the water is wound up the pump. It spurts out of the top and into a ditch or trough.

Think about it!

It might seem strange that a ship moves forward by pushing water backwards, but you do the same thing when you swim. How do you push the water backwards to move yourself forward through the water?

24

Propellers

A **propeller** is a kind of screw. The blades are curved and slanted. As they turn they **spiral** through the water and push the boat forward. The propellers are tiny compared with the size of the ship, but the action of these screws is so powerful that two propellers can drive a huge ship.

As the propellers on the back of the ship spin around, the blades push the water backward. This in turn pushes the ship forward.

The propeller turns clockwise to push the boat forward. The boat can be made to move backward by turning the propeller the other way. Since a boat does not have brakes, the quickest way to stop it is to turn the propellers into reverse.

Aircraft Propellers

The **propeller** on an aircraft works like the propeller on a ship. The blades are twisted so that, as they spin, they pull the aircraft through the air. They are turned by the engine, and screw through the air like a metal screw pushing into wood.

A propeller pulls this plane through the air. The propeller is turned by an engine.

Try this!

Cut a piece of paper and fold it as shown. Put a paper clip on the end. Now stand on a chair and drop the paper. What happens?

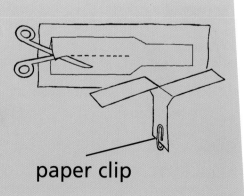

paper clip

The blades of the helicopter act like a propeller to move it through the air.

Helicopter

A helicopter has three or more large blades. The blades are wings as well as propellers. As they spin they keep the helicopter up and push it through the air.

Unlike an airplane, a helicopter can move backward and sideways as well as forward. The pilot changes direction by changing the tilt of the blades. Helicopters can move straight up and down so they can take off and land on a very small space.

A helicopter can also hover in one spot. They are often used to rescue people from ships or cliff faces. An ambulance helicopter can airlift people straight to a landing site on a hospital roof.

Make a Pinwheel

This toy uses a **propeller** that spins in the wind or when you blow on it. The propeller is a screw, and the toy will work best if you use a metal nail or pin to attach the propeller to the stick.

You will need:

- Stiff paper or thin cardboard
- Ruler
- Masking tape
- A stick at least 1/2 inch thick
- A small thin nail
- Pencil, scissors

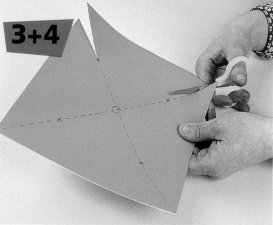

1   Draw a square 8 inches
    by 8 inches on the
    paper or cardboard.

2   Draw dotted lines that
    connect the opposite
    corners. Draw a small circle
    around the point where
    the two lines
    cross.

3   Use a ruler to measure along
    the dotted lines. Make a small cross at
    the halfway point between the circle in
    the middle and each corner.

4   Cut out the square and cut down each
    diagonal as far as the small cross.

5   Fold every other corner over so that it
    touches the outside of the center
    circle. Tape each corner down to
    make a propeller.

6   Place the propeller at the top of the
    stick. Push the nail through the
    center and into the wood to hold the propeller
    firmly in place. Make sure the propeller can
    spin freely.

7   Hold the toy in front of you and blow on the
    propeller. It should spin around.

Glossary

airtight made so that air cannot get in or out

auger large tool for boring holes and moving dirt, water, or rock out of holes

conveyor belt wide, flat loop that turns to carry something from one end to the other

drill tool for boring holes

drill bit spiral screw with a sharp point on the end of the drill

effort force applied to make something move

force push, pull, or twist that makes something move

hexagonal having six sides of equal length

hinge two metal plates joined together so they can swing open and closed

jack tool for lifting a heavy weight, such as a car

moldy covered with a fungus and beginning to rot

plasterboard board made of plaster and felt used to make walls inside a building

propeller curved blade that turns around to push a plane through the air or a boat through the water

pump machine for lifting water

screwdriver tool for driving a screw into wood or other material

seal something that fits so tightly neither gas nor liquid can get in or out

spiral slope that circles up or down

vise tool that uses a screw to hold something very tightly

washer flat ring that makes a tight seal in a tap

wrench tool for turning a nut on a bolt in order to loosen or tighten the nut

Answers to Questions

p. 9 If the lid of the pickles was loose and the jar was knocked over, the liquid would spill out. Also, the liquid might dry out and the pickles could go bad.

p. 11 The big bolt would fit the nut on the lower right. The longer thin bolt would fit the wing nut.

p. 11 The adjustable wrench uses a spiral thread, like a screw, to adjust the claw to the size of the nut.

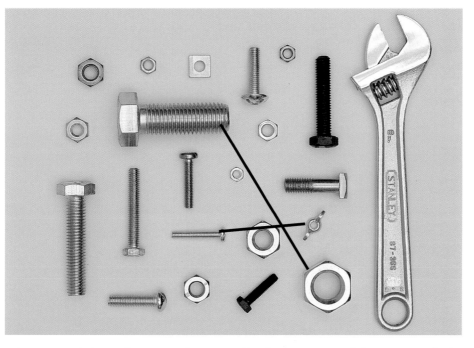

p. 11 The outside of a nut is usually hexagonal because it is easier to grip it with the wrench. If it were round, it would slip.

p. 15 Screws are made of metal because metal is strong. Wax and plaster would crumble.

p. 24 When you swim you pull the water backwards with your arms and push it backwards as you kick or move your feet and legs.

p. 26 The propeller spins as it drops. Notice that it always spins counterclockwise.

Index

More Books to Read

Grimshaw, Caroline. *Machines.* Chicago: World Book Inc., 1998.

Lafferty, Peter. *What's Inside Everyday Things?* Lincolnwood, IL: N.T.C. Contemporary Publishing, 1995.

Macaulay, David. *The Way Things Work 2.0.* New York: DK Publishing, Inc., 1997.